REMAIN
in Me...

CONTEMPLATIVE LIFE
IN THE WORLD

REMAIN
in Me...

CONTEMPLATIVE LIFE
IN THE WORLD

ANDREAS SCHMIDT

 Scepter

Scepter Publishers, Inc.
P.O. Box 211, New York, N.Y. 10018
www.scepterpublishers.org

Text design by Carol Sawyer/Rose Design

Printed in the United States of America

ISBN: 978 1 59417 145 1

Contents

Introduction

"Pray without ceasing!" (1 Thess 5:17).

What an enormous demand! On the one hand, what St. Paul tells the Christians of Thessalonica seems completely unrealistic. How could that be done today, with the thousand demands on our time from morning to night? "Pray all the time." Maybe a few monks could do that, living separated from the world as they do. But us?

On the other hand, Paul was not writing to a monastery, but to Christians living in the middle of the world. Perhaps we also perceive that prayer is something more than just sending a few words in the direction of heaven every now and then. The life of prayer is, as the *Catechism* tells us, "being in the presence of the thrice-holy God and in communion with him."[1]

That, after all, is our calling as Christians: to receive the love of God and to live by means of it, not just from time to time, but in every moment of our life. To "pray without ceasing" or the "contemplative life" signifies nothing other than living every moment in the presence of God and never separating ourselves from his love. The question is how.

---

1. *Catechism of the Catholic Church* no. 2565, hereafter cited as CCC.

It often happens that everyday life, with all of its demands, overwhelms us, so that we do not succeed in remaining in contact with God—even though we really want to do so and make an effort. Is "pray without ceasing" therefore an unattainable goal?

Jesus himself taught his disciples that they "ought always to pray" (Lk 18:1), and we know he doesn't demand things of us that are impossible right from the start. What the Old Testament says about the Torah is also applicable to the words of Jesus: "This commandment which I command you this day is not too hard for you, neither is it far off" (Deut 18:1). And the *Catechism* encourages us: "It is always possible to pray" (*Catechism of the Catholic Church* 2743).

This little book is about how to succeed "in living contemplatively," that is, in making life more and more a "prayer without ceasing." In speaking about this, I shall base what I say on, among other things, the *Catechism of the Catholic Church*, whose fourth part is devoted entirely to the subject of prayer, and on the guidelines left for us by the great teachers of prayer.

Chapter 1

THE UNIVERSAL CALL TO CONTEMPLATIVE LIFE

1. What is "contemplative life"?

The word "contemplative" has different meanings. The Latin word "*contemplari*" means to look at something, to consider it. The spiritual sense is an inner consideration of something: mysteries of the faith or simply God himself. First of all, though, contemplative life is a way of life in which I do not lose sight of God, but—as the psalms put it—keep him "always before me" (Ps 16:8).

Starting with this basic meaning, "contemplative" is used in different ways. "Contemplative orders" are religious orders that follow a life of solitude and silence in order to devote themselves entirely to prayer. "Contemplation" also stands for a particular kind of prayer, namely, the silent inner prayer that, according to the *Catechism*, takes place in "the pre-eminently intense time of prayer" (CCC 2714). In a broader sense, though, contemplative life means the life of prayer in general: a life in constant union with God. This is its sense in this book unless otherwise specified.

Contemplative life offers us a key to the Christian life. If we think of faith as just accepting certain truths or observing certain moral laws, we haven't gotten to the root of the matter. "Abide in me, and I in you" (Jn 15:4). Where Jesus is concerned, it's a matter of unity of life, life in an ever-deeper union of love with him and through him with the Triune God. In this sense, whether living in a secluded cloister or in the middle of the world, we are all called to contemplative life.

"Even as thou, Father, art in me, and I in thee, that they also may be in us" (Jn 17:21). According to the model of Trinitarian love between the Father and Son, we also should be one with Jesus and, through him and in the Holy Spirit, one with the Father. Love in its highest perfection, in the Trinity, leads to mutual being-in-another, i.e., being completely given to the other and at the same time constantly receiving the other in oneself. It is to a union in love like this that Jesus calls us.

Contemplative life means directing one's heart toward Christ in every moment, keeping the heart always open and ready to receive him, his light and his love, and the Holy Spirit, who streams from him without ceasing—and this not only in the time of prayer but in all ones does. Contemplative life means—as the Fathers of the Church, reflecting on the Gospel, have pointed out—combining the spirit of Martha with that of Mary: remaining unreservedly close to our Lord and resting at his feet even when one is busy in outward activities (cf. Lk 10:38–42).

2. God lives in us

"If a man loves me, he will keep my word, and my Father will love him, and we will come to him and make our home with him" (Jn 14:23). We are dwelling places of the Most Blessed Trinity. As a consequence of baptism, the Triune God lives within us.

The saints speak of the vivid experience of God's presence in us. St. Augustine writes: "You were within me and I was outside of myself and sought you there . . . You were with me but I was not with you."[1] In the sixteenth century, Teresa of Avila took these words and added: "There where God is, is heaven. Consider, therefore, what St. Augustine said, who sought God everywhere and found Him within himself. . . . It seems to me, if I had grasped, as I do today, that in this tiny palace of my soul such a great King lives, then I would not have left him alone so often, and would have stayed with him from time to time."[2]

Teresa speaks of the soul as "the inner royal palace." Dwelling in this inner place is the Most Holy Trinity; and the way of prayer is a way that goes deeper and deeper into the soul, to where God lives and invites us to share in his Triune life.[3] "God's love has been poured into our hearts through the

---

1. St. Augustine, *Confessions*, Ch. 10.

2. St. Teresa of Avila, *Way of Perfection*, 28, 2.

3. This is not to be confused with the "Pseudo-mysticism" that is rather widespread today, somewhat in the form of "I have to find myself, and when I am fully with myself, I will be fully with God." That is a false identification of one's own ego with God, often an idea taken from oriental religions under the influence of esoteric ideas. Where it is only a matter of such a search for one's own "self," there can't be any love, since love always requires two persons

Holy Spirit which has been given to us" (Rom 5:5). Through
the Holy Spirit given to us in baptism, God lives in us. He is
the source of divine life. "The water that I shall give him will
become in him a spring of water welling up to eternal life"
(Jn 4:14). Contemplative life is the art of continually drink-
ing from this ever-flowing source. The Holy Spirit "bubbles
up" *in* us, but all too often—and in vain—we seek *outside* for
the water that will quench our thirst. Without a link to this
inner fountain, life dries up. Contemplative life, then, is life
that comes forth from the Holy Spirit dwelling within us. The
Holy Spirit is the Spirit of love of the Father and the Son. He
is the constant reception of love and self-giving in love. He
leads us into the community of life and love of the Triune
God, and enables us to remain there.

3. We live in the Triune God

"Abide in me, and I in you" (Jn 15:4). God lives in us, but we
also live in God. That is true not just after death but also now.
To abide in Jesus, and through him in the love of the Triune
God, is heaven. Yes, only in eternal life will this oneness in
love will be perfected, but even now it is real.

The basis having been laid in baptism, we enter in prayer
into this spiritual reality of life in the Triune God. "The grace
of the Kingdom of God is 'the union of the entire holy and

---

differentiated from one another. But the one dwelling in me is the one who is
completely "other" and yet who wants to have the deepest community of love
with me. And when I do become one with him, then I have really found myself.
Then I have reached the goal for which God has created me: to live the deepest unity of love, but without losing my own identity.

royal Trinity . . . with the whole human spirit' (Gregory of Nazianzus, or. 16, 9). Thus, the life of prayer is the habit of being in the presence of the thrice-holy God and in communion with him" (CCC 2565). In contemplative life, then, we already have a share in the life of heaven. God has "raised us up with him, and made us sit with him in the heavenly places in Christ Jesus" (Eph 2:6). Notice the past tense. This is something that has already happened!

In no way does taking this truth of faith seriously distance us from life in this world. Living in heaven does not conflict to being wholly in the world. Quite the opposite, for living in God's heart inserts us into the very heart of the world. If we are filled with God's love, we love together with him. The more united in love we are with God, the more we share his longing for "all men to be saved and to come to the knowledge of the truth" (1 Tim 2:4). Compassion and a thirst to evangelize arise from prayer,[4] whereas without contemplative life it is all too easy to draw back into the isolated world of one's own egotism. On the other hand, life "in Christ with every spiritual blessing in the heavenly places" (Eph 1:3) draws us out of egotism to an encounter with those who need our love and the proclamation of the word.

4. Contemplative life is possible

"Pray constantly!" (1 Thess 5:17). We are tempted to think at once, "That's impossible." Maybe we even tried it for a while, but the demands and distractions of daily life compelled us

---

4. From the Preamble to the Statutes of the Community of Emmanuel.

constantly to turn aside from our interior recollection of God's presence. Now we suppose we aren't capable of any such continuous prayer. And so we give up on it.

Teresa of Avila reports that she completely gave up interior prayer for more than a year because she felt unworthy of it. Here is another temptation. But our Lord does not stop tugging at us, even though we distance ourselves from him again and again.

Now as a matter of fact, by ourselves we really are incapable of continuous prayer. Jesus tells us that quite clearly: "Apart from me you can do nothing" (Jn 15:5). But the Gospel also says: "With God nothing will be impossible" (Lk 1:37).

At the beginning of the *Itinerarium mentis in Deum* (*The Way of the Spirit to God*) St. Bonaventure makes the point that to live contemplatively, we must, among other things, have a longing for it. "No one, then, is in any way ready for God-given contemplation if he is not, like Daniel, a 'man of desires'" (Dan 10:11, Douai-Rheims translation).[5] Desire, or longing, is the key.

In the Song of Songs the bride asks her beloved: "Draw me after you, let us make haste" (Song 1:4). St. Gregory remarks of this that "one who says 'draw me' is referring to something that he wants and something that he cannot do."[6] We can't produce contemplative life at will, but we can long for it, and our Lord will not let our urgent longing go unanswered. In

5. Bonaventure, *Itinerarium mentis in Deum*, Prologue no. 3. In *Theologie der Spiritualität, Quellentexte*, published by the Institute for Spirituality, Munster, Vol. 3, 7.

6. Gregory the Great, Exegesis of the Song of Songs, no. 24. Cit. by K. Suso Frank: *Gregor der Grosse und Origenes, Das Hohelied*, 111–112.

the very next verse the bride calls out, "The king has brought me into his chambers." Of this the monk Nilus says: "God leads the soul that longs for him into his inner mystery, into his heart."[7] Through our own strength we are incapable of contemplative life, but when we long for it wholeheartedly and ask God for it, he then raises us up onto "the rock that is too high for us" (cf. Ps 61:2).

To live the contemplative life in its fullness one needn't withdraw from the world. To be sure, there is such a thing as the calling to life in a contemplative religious order. And a life lived that way does indeed affect the world through prayer and sacrifice. But most of us live squarely in the world and Jesus' words about praying constantly are also directed to us. And if he says it, then we know it is possible. But how? How can we really be contemplative in the midst of ordinary life?

To answer this question it's necessary first to look at the prerequisites for prayer, then at the time of prayer itself, and then at everyday life—the environment in which we must pray.

---

7. Cf. Prokop–*Catene zum Hld*, PG 87, Sp 1552.

Chapter 2

PREREQUISITES FOR PRAYER

Prayer can't be separated from the way one lives one's daily life. "We pray as we live, because we live as we pray" (CCC 2725). It's not enough merely to pray and let life take its course. To pray correctly, one must direct one's whole life to God.

Whatever we can do on our own to take up prayer can be called—in classic terminology—"the asceticism of prayer." This asceticism—our human effort, that is—is an expression of our longing. It shows our Lord that we are serious about wanting to pray constantly. It is not a method that leads automatically to a desired goal, but a cry of longing for God.

God alone can give us the grace of a life of prayer, but for this he awaits our cry of longing. St. Thérèse of Lisieux expressed the connection by an image. A child wants to climb a flight of stairs, but isn't able to mount even the first step because he's too small. Waiting at the top of the stairs, however, is his father. When the father sees the child trying to climb the stairs, he comes to meet him and raises the child to himself.

1. Determination

The *Catechism* stresses that prayer always marks a "determined response" (CCC 2725) on our part to the gift of God. Specifically: "The choice of the time and duration of the prayer arises from a determined will, revealing the secrets of the heart. One does not undertake contemplative prayer only when one has the time: one makes time for the Lord, with the firm determination not to give up, no matter what trials and dryness one may encounter" (CCC 2710).[1]

If we let ourselves be governed by feelings and moods, we shall soon abandon the way of prayer. To continue on the path of prayer even when it is hard requires a deeply rooted act of will. St. Teresa of Avila calls this the most important precondition. "To the question of how one should begin on this path, I can only answer: It is important above all, it is in fact indispensable, to begin with strong determination and then not to stop until one has reached the goal, and to do this, whatever may happen, whatever we may encounter, even when the effort becomes extremely great or when others gossip about us."[2]

This determination is therefore especially important when one must struggle with difficulties in one's prayer life, whether

---

1. Cf. St. Teresa of Avila, *The Way of Perfection*, 23, 2: "Since we have resolved to devote to him this very brief period of time . . . let us give it to him, entirely resolved never to take it back again, whatever we may suffer through trials, annoyances, or aridities."

2. Ibid., 20, 2. This determination is often accompanied by a real battle. Teresa passionately called her sisters to this battle: "Do not stop in the way, but battle like strong women, fight till there is blood. Go your way with the determination to die rather than to give up your goal, even if the Lord allows you to suffer great thirst in this life."

these are external or internal. This determination is needed if one is to continue on the way of prayer, holding fast to the daily time of prayer and not being led astray.

2. Longing for holiness

The Second Vatican Council defined holiness as the perfection of charity and taught that all Christians are called to holiness.[3] There is a deep inner connection between holiness of life and the life of prayer. Or, as St. Teresa put it: "Prayer and a soft life don't go together." To undertake contemplative life, one must have a longing for holiness. That doesn't mean one must be a saint before beginning to pray. It means one must long to be holy and strive for it.

Holiness means, first of all, living love of neighbor in a concrete way. Love of neighbor leads directly to a relationship of love with God, that is, into prayer. In the words of Pope Benedict: "If in my life I fail completely to heed others . . . then my relationship with God will also grow arid. Only my readiness to encounter my neighbor and to show him love makes me sensitive to God as well."[4]

Besides love of neighbor, the holiness to which God is calling us is made concrete in a large number of other virtues like justice, prudence, temperance, self-control, kindness, friendliness, trustworthiness, etc. Prayer and virtues influence one another. Growth in virtue is among the fruits of prayer. But at the same time it is necessary to strive for virtues as strongly as

---

3. Cf. Vatican II, Constitution *Lumen Gentium*, Ch. 5.
4. Pope Benedict XVI, Encyclical *Deus Caritas Est*, no. 18.

we can so that our prayer will be genuine and deep. St. Teresa wrote: "The King of glory will not come into our soul—to unite with us, I mean—if we are not struggling to grow in the virtues."[5]

Striving for holiness involves not only practicing virtue but overcoming vice. "Blessed are the pure in heart, for they shall see God" (Mt 5:8). A clean conscience is a prerequisite of clear-sightedness in the spiritual realm. Like an extremely dirty windshield that makes it hard to drive a car, sin obscures our 'vision' of God. Regular reception of the Sacrament of Reconciliation thus contributes to a deeper prayer life. It's a common experience that prayer is very different after a good confession: what blocked the relationship with God has been cleared away, and prayer is easier and deeper.

To repeat: one need not be perfect in order to pray. The two things are joined in love for God. We yearn for holiness and also for a life of prayer. Prayer and holiness cannot be separated. They stem from the same love.

3. Inner freedom

Here, too, we see a very substantial prerequisite for prayer: inner freedom in relation to earthly goods. St. Teresa advised her sisters: "Care nothing for any created things, but embrace the Creator alone."[6] This doesn't mean undervaluing or rejecting creatures or created goods, but not being attached to them or thinking our entire fulfillment depends on them.

---

5. Teresa of Avila, *The Way of Perfection*, 16, 2.
6. Ibid., 8, 1.

Of friendship, for instance, St. Teresa said: "We thank the Creator for a friend, but to see fulfillment in him—no!"[7]

In a way, it can all be summed up in a question: Where—to what or to whom—do I look for my deepest and most genuine happiness? We need to make a realistic evaluation of earthly goods like human relationships, material possessions, hobbies, and the rest. They are gifts of the Creator, grounds for joy over the divine goodness that is reflected in them. But by themselves they cannot satisfy our deepest longings for fulfillment and happiness. Original sin is the source of the deep-rooted human error of exchanging God's truth for a lie, of honoring creatures and worshiping them rather than the one who made them (cf. Rom 1:25).

The modern mind is too focused on the present. Many people seek their happiness exclusively in the goods of this world. We must be very careful not to be infected by this mindset, for all of us have the "old man" in us, and the current of the times easily carries us along with it. Yet the engine driving all earthly wishes—whether we know it or not—is at bottom a longing for God. Original sin makes our longing skewed and off-target—it simply doesn't reach far enough. Instead it focuses on worldly goods that can never give us the fulfillment we desire.

For us to have inner freedom, the longing of our hearts must once more be expanded and directed toward God, the giver of all earthly gifts. "I say to the Lord, 'Thou art my Lord; I have no good apart from thee'" (Ps 16:2). "For me it is good to be near God" (Ps 73:28)—and nothing else can give this

---

7. Ibid., 6, 4.

happiness. "My soul clings to thee" (Ps 63:8)—and to no earthly good. When we understand this deep in our hearts, we will be free.

Then, in fact, and only then, we will be free to enjoy earthly goods as they should be enjoyed![8] Edith Stein wrote: "One who frees himself from all attachment to temporal goods, will attain freedom of the spirit, clarity of understanding, deep calm, and peaceful trust in God. One will even find more joy in creatures through renunciation: a joy that the covetous cannot taste, because in their restiveness they lack the necessary spiritual freedom. The person who is free discovers in goods their true natural and supernatural value."[9]

The cardinal virtue of temperance is essential to a correct attitude toward created goods. Its theme is a proper balance in regard to everything. Inner freedom thus combines gratitude for the gifts of the Creator with a certain equanimity and detachment: I am pleased by them, but not too attached to or overly desirous of them. Above all, our joy in earthly goods is directed to the one who gives them to us: we accept God's gifts with gratitude and praise. "For everything created by God is good, and nothing is to be rejected if it is received with thanksgiving" (1 Tim 4:4). In gratitude we look from gift to giver. In giving praise, we consider the goodness and love that are the sources of his gifts.

---

8. For the word of God calls us to this also: "If a man is mean to himself, to whom will he be generous? He will not enjoy his own riches. . . . Do not deprive yourself of a happy day; let not your share of desired good pass by you" (Sir 14:5, 14).

9. Edith Stein, *Gesamtausgabe*, Freiburg im Breisgau, 2003, vol. 18, *Kreuzeswissenschaft* (*The Science of the Cross*), 77.

The Church fathers called this inner freedom "freedom from the passions" (*apatheia*). The passions in biblical parlance were understood as a kind of compulsive craving for earthly goods. They are something we "experience" or "suffer"; we don't control them, they control us. They exercise an inner constraint on us.

Jesus frees us from this compulsive craving. "For freedom Christ has set us free. . . . And those who belong to Christ Jesus have crucified the flesh with its passions and desires. If we live by the Spirit, let us also walk by the Spirit" (Gal 5:1, 24–25). Jesus knows that earthly goods will not fully satisfy the soul, since its desires go much deeper. "Every one who drinks of this water will thirst again, but whoever drinks of the water that I shall give him will never thirst; the water that I shall give him will become in him a spring of water welling up to eternal life" (Jn 4:13–14). The more we accept the Holy Spirit and live by him, the freer we become.

Desires and passions are not conquered by battling them and trying to repress them. That can have just the opposite effect. Instead, think of the sun and the moon. As the light of day becomes stronger, the moon becomes dimmer. In like manner, the more the light of Christ fills our lives, the more these desires lose their power over us. "The heart becomes filled with heavenly comfort, next to which all joys and pleasures of the world pale. In this way the soul is made ready to turn with all its strength away from earthly goods and to raise itself to the heavenly."[10]

_____

10. Ibid., 99.

Inner freedom is a fruit of life in the Holy Spirit. Our contribution lies in letting God release us slowly and gently from attachments. As we live with Christ, much that earlier appeared indispensable takes on a very different significance: We still find it attractive, but without being attached to it. Inner freedom is a help to prayer, and prayer enables us to grow in inner freedom.

4. Surrender to God

Blessed Charles de Foucauld has left us a prayer that expresses surrender to God in simple, deeply penetrating words: "Father, I abandon myself into your hands; do with me what you will. Whatever you may do, I thank you: I am ready for all, I accept all. Let only your will be done in me, and in all your creatures. I wish no more than this, O Lord. Into your hands I commend my soul; I offer it to you with all the love of my heart, for I love you, Lord, and so need to give myself, to surrender myself into your hands, without reserve, and with boundless confidence, for you are my Father."[11]

As this prayer makes clear, self-surrender is possible only in faith. God knows me much better than I know myself. He loves me much more than I do. He knows best what is good for me. Faith in him allows me to surrender myself, to give myself over to his will. I can still offer petitions to the Lord. But I do it knowing that his thoughts are not our thoughts, his ways not ours (cf. Is 55:8).

---

11. *Gotteslob*, 5, 5. (Prayer and hymn book for all German dioceses.)

This self-surrender or abandonment contains a further prerequisite for prayer. "I cannot pray and want to hold onto myself."[12] St. Teresa of Avila stressed this strongly. "The King only gives himself to those who also give themselves entirely to him. That is certainly so, and because it is a very important point, I remind you of it again and again. God cannot operate in many souls as he would if they gave themselves to him fully and without reservation."[13] And in another place: "When we do not give our will entirely to our Lord, so that he, in all that concerns us, can act according to his will, he will never allow us to drink the living water from the fountain. That water is perfect contemplation."[14]

Without perfect abandonment, one can never enter into deeper prayer. Abandonment means placing God and his will first in one's life. The prayer that Jesus taught is a prayer of abandonment: "Our Father . . . thy will be done." True prayer exists only in this spirit of abandonment.

Abandonment also means learning to let go of one's own will. Often, even in prayer, we cling to our own will, our agenda, our idea of how our life should proceed and our list of things we want from God. In such "prayer," God is no more than someone who should do our will. And in this manner we put ourselves, in a sense, in God's place. When he does not give us what we want, we are disappointed and give up praying. This may be why so many never go deeper in prayer. The only kind of prayer they've learned is petition—asking God to do as they will.

12. Cf. P. H. Buob, *Tür nach innen*, Hochaltingen 2004, 19.
13. Teresa of Avila, *The Way of Perfection*, 15, 4 and 28, 12.
14. Ibid., 32, 8.

The spirit of abandonment is directly opposed to this: "Thy will be done"—not my will! By this abandonment people open the door to God to act in their lives. Such abandonment does not occur once and for all; it must be constantly renewed and deepened. Especially when encountering something difficult, one can be tempted to cancel one's abandonment, as it were. Often, too, abandonment is very imperfect. One hands over this while holding on to that. Eventually God will show us what one remains attached to and will help one hand over to him the whole of life not just parts of it.

Resolution, inner freedom, longing for holiness, abandonment—the more these inner attitudes grow in us, the more open and ready we will be for prayer. But for the life of prayer to grow out of these attitudes, we must devote regular periods of time to prayer alone. We'll look at that in the next chapter.

Chapter 3

THE TIME OF PRAYER

The *Catechism* gets right to the point: "We cannot pray 'at all times' if we do not pray at specific times, consciously willing it. These are the special times of Christian prayer, both in intensity and duration" (CCC 2697).

1. Beginning the time of prayer—recollection

How the time of prayer begins is crucial. All too often people start to speak interiorly. Or they allow their thoughts to follow whatever passes through their minds. Neither thing is conducive to the close personal relationship that is prayer's whole purpose.

It's essential at the start to "recollect oneself," as the traditional expression has it, that is, to become aware of whom one is speaking with. St. Teresa offers this comparison: If we had an audience with the king, we would carefully consider what we were going to say to him;[1] but when we come before

---

1. Ibid., 22, 1.

the King of Heaven, how little we consider in whose presence we find ourselves! The *Catechism* describes the beginning of prayer like this: "We 'gather up' the heart, recollect our whole being under the prompting of the Holy Spirit, abide in the dwelling place of the Lord which we are, awaken our faith in order to enter into the presence of him who awaits us" (CCC 2711).

Much distraction in prayer comes by skipping this first step, recollection, and speaking to God as if he were far away. Recollection means becoming conscious that God is *present*. I am now in his presence—in the presence of the Triune God, who loves me. I am not just "facing God," to ask for things and thank him. I am invited, so to speak, to take my place in the Trinity,[2] through Jesus Christ, the beloved son of the Father, and in the Holy Spirit. Recollection means entering by an act of faith into this spiritual reality of divine filiation, which is granted to us through baptism. No matter how distracted or tired we may be, it is always possible to enter through a conscious act of faith into inner companionship with God. Even an act of faith made without any great feeling unites us directly with God and leads us into the eternal community of love among the Father, Son, and Holy Spirit. "He who believes has eternal life" (Jn 6:47).

To fully become part of this relationship of love requires the help of the Holy Spirit. It is above all through him that the act of faith comes alive. He leads us into a dialogue of love between Father and Son and enables us to pray as true

---

2. The well-known Trinitarian icon of Andrei Rublev suggests this place that is prepared for us with the Blessed Trinity.

children of God. The Spirit calls out within us, "*Abba*, Father" (Rom 8:15). Thus it also is part of recollection to call upon the Holy Spirit, to rely fully on his support, and to unite ourselves with the one who is praying within us. "'No one can say "Jesus is Lord" except by the Holy Spirit' (1 Cor 12:3). Every time that we begin to pray to Jesus it is the Holy Spirit who draws us on the way of prayer by his prevenient grace" (CCC 2670).

Recollection is easier if we can pray before the Blessed Sacrament and consider Christ present in the Host. The consecrated Host helps us be aware of the presence of God and assume a personal "I-Thou" relationship with him. But even then we can slip into self-centered prayer—in which it is time to renew the I-Thou relationship.

Christ in the Eucharist leads us into the community of the Triune God: "In the Eucharist we find ourselves in the current that draws us into the blessed presence of the Father. The Eucharistic Lord is the Christ who has been offered up, who died and has risen, and thus takes us into this movement—away from ourselves and towards the Father—with him. Thus we are brought into this upward flow that brings us above ourselves into the thought of the Father, into the will of the Father and into the love of the Father."[3]

2. Kinds of prayer

Prayer is love, and love can never be reduced to a system. It would not be possible to bring the teachings of Church fathers and saints like Sts. John of the Cross, Francis de Sales,

---

3. From the homily of Cardinal Joachim Meisner to the Autumn Assembly of the German Bishops, 2005.

and Ignatius Loyola into a single system, since the experiences they describe are too personally colored. "To be sure, there are as many paths of prayer as there are persons who pray" (CCC 2672). The ways of prayer are always surprising, an adventure of love with our Lord. "The Lord leads all persons by paths and in ways pleasing to him" (CCC 2699). Thus the most important lesson in regard to the life of prayer is to let oneself be led by the Holy Spirit. "The Holy Spirit, whose anointing permeates our whole being, is the interior Master of Christian prayer" (CCC 2672).

There is, nevertheless, a rich treasure of spiritual teaching about prayer in the tradition of the Church. In one way or another, everyone who travels the path of prayer meets up with certain developments, difficulties, and experiences. These recurring experiences, which the saints describe, can also help us. Thus the *Catechism* also says, "One must also learn how to pray" (CCC 2650). Even though the real teacher of prayer is the Holy Spirit himself, we need help and guidance to discover the full wealth of prayer.

The *Catechism* speaks of "three major expressions of prayer": vocal, meditative, and contemplative (CCC 2699). We shall use this division in considering the path of prayer in greater detail.

Vocal prayer (*oratio*). "Vocal prayer" refers to everything that can be formulated in words: spoken or silent requests, thanks, praise. Ordinarily we practice vocal prayer the same way both in personal and communal prayer. Vocal prayer "is an essential element of the Christian life" (CCC 2701). It is not just a "beginner's method" that is later left behind in favor of meditative and contemplative prayer exclusively. The *Catechism* says: "Even interior prayer . . . cannot neglect vocal prayer" (CCC 2704). As we shall see, the *Catechism's* "three major expressions of prayer" work together.

In regard to vocal prayer the *Catechism* stresses that "it is most important that the heart should be present to him to whom we are speaking" (CCC 2700). God wants us to honor him not only with our lips but with our hearts, and not "while their hearts are far from me" (Is 29:13). Vocal prayer requires one to struggle to grasp the meaning of what is being prayed or sung and to bring it before God as the prayer of one's heart.

The intellect is one dimension but only one. More than anything else praying is a matter of the will. In the biblical sense the "heart" with which we should pray refers to both: it is the deepest core of the human person, illumined by the intellect and moved by the will. The words of the hymn, "My Father, I give myself to you," speak of a decision of the will. It's of little use to sing the song for its catchy melody without confirming this act of self-giving with one's will.

Vocal prayer, according to the *Catechism*, suits our human nature, made up as it is of body and soul (cf. CCC 2702). We express our prayer in a bodily manner, in words and at times also in gestures. Spoken, the prayer fills our intellect, our feelings, our imagination, and our body. If we never prayed out loud, prayer would be in some way weakened. There is interaction between soul and body, and praying bodily strengthens the soul. For this reason, vocal prayer is especially important in difficult times—times of physical exhaustion, sickness, or spiritual dryness. In those cases only vocal prayer often is all that's possible. Thérèse of Lisieux reports how much help she found in times of inner dryness in simply saying an Our Father slowly (with her whole heart). The monk Siloan advises: "When you want to pray with your heart, but cannot do this, say the prayer with your lips and keep your spirit fastened to the words of the prayer. The Lord will in time give you the intimacy of prayer."

Vocal prayer is also important for 'broadening' personal prayer. Familiar prayers like the prayer of St. Francis of Assisi, "Lord, make me an instrument of your peace," help us put the longings of our hearts into words we haven't found on our own. The prayer of abandonment of Charles de Foucauld, "Father, I abandon myself into your hands," offers a challenge by inviting us to an abandonment to God perhaps going beyond anything up to then prayed in our own words.

We need vocal prayer then. It nourishes and strengthens the spirit. But it needs to be fleshed out through meditation and inner prayer. Otherwise it remains external and without great effect on life.

Meditative prayer (*meditatio*). "Meditation is above all a quest. The mind seeks to understand the why and how of the Christian life, in order to adhere and respond to what the Lord is asking. The required attentiveness is difficult to sustain. We are usually helped by books, and Christians do not want for them: the Sacred Scriptures, particularly the Gospels, holy icons, liturgical texts of the day or season, writings of the spiritual fathers, works of spirituality, the great book of creation, and that of history, the page on which the 'today' of God is written" (CCC 2705).

As this suggests, meditation is a broader concept. One thinks perhaps about a word of Holy Scripture or one of the mysteries of the life of Jesus (for example, those considered in the Rosary) or about the connection between different truths of faith. Sometimes it can be 'dry,' purely an effort of the mind. Other times it is experienced as a gift: one suddenly sees some passage of the Bible in a new light, with previously unperceived depth. Or one suddenly grasps a sentence of the creed inwardly.

If understood more deeply, a truth of faith moves us more interiorly. It stirs our feelings and our will and inflames our love for God. Meditation is thus not only a matter of growing in understanding, but also of increasing in love. The Spiritual Exercises of St. Ignatius are a classic example of meditative prayer in which Ignatius invites someone making them to put himself into the life of Jesus with all his power of imagination. We are to "ponder and test" what the Gospel tells us. Only thus can the word of God reach not only the understanding but also the heart, and finally move the will. That is the goal of meditation: to have an effect on the decisions of the will, so that we may be "doers of the word, and not hearers only" (cf. Jas 1:22).

St. Edith Stein describes meditative prayer in this manner: "Here one's imaginative power puts the events of the history of salvation before one's eyes in a pictorial way, seeks to exhaustively consider them with all one's senses, evaluates with the intellect their general meaning and the demands that they place on one. Thereby the will is excited to love, and to resolutions for bringing one's life into conformity with the spirit of faith."[4] Using the example of the mystery of the birth of Jesus, she points out: "The imagination (of man) puts him in the cave of Bethlehem, shows him the child in the crib, his parents, the shepherds, and magi. The intellect considers the greatness of the divine mercy, the mind is taken by love and gratitude, the will makes resolutions to make itself more worthy of God's love. In this way, meditation requires all of the powers of the soul, and, with real persistence, it gradually changes the whole person."[5]

In the Angelus, to which church bells summon us three times during the day, we have an opportunity to meditate on these truths of the faith. So too with the mysteries of the Rosary. Here are reminders that vocal prayer attains its full depth only when it is done meditatively.

In meditation I enter into some scene in the Bible. I am with the little group in the stable of Bethlehem. I am present at one of Jesus' encounters with sick people or with tax collectors and sinners. I am there at the way of the cross and on Calvary. I witness a meeting with the risen Christ. I am with the disciples as they await the coming of the Holy Spirit. I try to imagine the scene in a lively way, for example, Jesus speaking with the adulteress. I can see the faces of the onlookers, the woman's face, the faces of the accusers, Jesus' face. I try to share the feelings of the different people. I try to imagine the impact on the adulteress of Jesus' words: "Neither do I condemn you; go, and do not sin again" (Jn 8:11). I imagine

---

4. Edith Stein, *Kreuzeswissenschaft* (*Science of the Cross*), op. cit., 96.
5. Edith Stein, *Das Kreuz wie eine Krone tragen* (*Wearing the Cross like a Crown*), Zürich, 1997, 105.

Jesus looking at me with the same look of infinite kindness
and mercy that knows everything yet instead of condemning
forgives, raises one up, and restores one's dignity. Meditation
should lead us to a dialogue with Jesus: "Lord, thank you for
not condemning me either. Thank you for having looked at
me with that look filled with kindness and mercy! Help me to
believe in your mercy and accept it for myself."

The *Catechism* lists among the "books" for meditation not
only the Holy Scripture and other religious texts, but also "the
great book of creation, and that of history the page on which
the 'today' of God is written" (CCC 2705).

God speaks to me through creation, through the people I
live with, through the events I experience. It is not necessarily
a distraction from meditation to look at my day—at situations
that arise, or tasks that lie before me. Lingering over these
things is a danger of course. But when, gazing at them, I refer
them to the Lord, that is meditative prayer in the best sense.
"Lord, what did you want to tell me through this? What is
your will in this situation? What should I do?" In prayer, especially the prayer of someone living an active life, there will
normally be times to look at one's life along with our Lord in
order to see it as he does and in relation to him. This is necessary so that the Holy Spirit can enlighten and guide us in the
decisions of everyday life, both great and small.

Meditative prayer is indispensable to Christian life. The
Catechism says: "Christians owe it to themselves to develop
the desire to meditate regularly, lest they come to resemble
the three first kinds of soil in the parable of the sower"
(CCC 2707). In case you've forgotten, those were soil by
the wayside where birds ate the seed, rocky soil where the

seeds couldn't put down roots, and soil filled with weeds that choked the seeds.

Meditation leads prayer into the deep. But the full depths of prayer are still not plumbed. "Christian prayer should go further: to the knowledge of the love of the Lord Jesus, to union with him" (CCC 2708). In other words: interior prayer.

Interior prayer (*contemplatio*). The *Catechism* refers to interior prayer as "the high point of prayer as a whole." The sections of the *Catechism* dealing with it (2709–2719) are among the densest and richest in content.

The essence of interior prayer

Let's begin with the definition of St. Teresa of Avila: "Mental prayer is nothing else, in my opinion, but being on terms of friendship with God, frequently conversing in secret with him who, we know, loves us."[6]

St. Francis de Sales sees interior prayer in similar terms: "Prayer is nothing else but a conversation in which the soul amorously entertains herself with God concerning his most amiable goodness, to unite and join herself thereto."[7] This meeting with God, according to Francis, is made up of "many different interior movements."[8] For "love speaks not only by the tongue, but by the eyes, by sighs, and play of features; yea, silence and dumbness are words for it."[9] Thus Francis calls

---

6. Teresa of Avila, *Life*, 8:5.
7. Francis de Sales, *Treatise on the Love of God*, Bk. 6, Ch. 1, art. 6.
8. Ibid., art. 2.
9. Ibid., art. 9.

interior prayer the "dialogue of silence": "Eyes speak to eyes, and heart to heart, and none understand what passes save the sacred lovers who speak."[10] This kind of quiet internal prayer is "contemplative" prayer in a narrower sense.

"In this inner prayer we can still meditate" (CCC 2709). But its essence is simply gazing upon Jesus. (cf. CCC 2709). "Contemplation is a gaze of faith, fixed on Jesus. 'I look at him and he looks at me'" (CCC 2715).[11]

Vocal prayer has a place in interior prayer, but in a completely new, much deeper way: "Words in this kind of prayer are not speeches; they are like kindling that feeds the fire of love" (CCC 2717). St. Francis could spend an entire day of prayer just repeating the first two words of the Lord's Prayer: "Our Father"!

Paths to interior prayer

According to St. Francis de Sales, meditation serves "to gather the love of God, but having gathered it we contemplate God, and are attentive to his goodness, by reason of the sweetness which love makes us find in it. The desire we have to obtain divine love makes us meditate, but love obtained makes us contemplate."[12] Meditation is therefore a path to contemplation: "To attain unto contemplation we stand ordinarily in need of hearing the word of God, of having spiritual discourse

---

10. Ibid.

11. Compare also the definition of Francis de Sales: Meditation considers things that are suitable to move us separately and together piece by piece. In contrast, contemplation grasps with a simple all-encompassing glance the thing that she loves.

12. *Treatise on the Love of God*, Bk. VI, Ch. 3, art. 1.

and conference with others . . . of reading, praying, meditating, singing canticles, conceiving good thoughts; holy contemplation being the end and aim of all these exercises."[13]

Humanly speaking, meditation corresponds to the process by which two people get acquainted, contemplation to their simply being together in love. The more deeply people get to know each other, the sooner they will reach this stage of simple unity.

St. Edith Stein described it like this: "The spirit—and that means not just the intellect but also the heart—becomes intimate through continuing engagement with God, he knows and loves him. This knowledge and love become a part of his being, something like the relationship with someone with whom one has lived for a long time and is on close terms. Such people do not need to get information about one another and think about one another, in order to understand each other and be convinced about their kindness. They hardly need to say a word to each other. Every time they are together there is a new wakefulness and a growth of love, perhaps even a growth of knowledge of some detail, but since that happens by itself, one need not concern oneself with it. Something like this is the relationship of a soul with God after long practice in the spiritual life. One doesn't have to look at him to know and love God. The path lies far behind one, one rests in the goal. As soon as one begins to pray, one is already with God and one rests in loving abandonment in his presence. One's silence is more attractive to him than many words."[14]

---

13. Ibid., Ch. 6, art. 5.
14. Edith Stein, *Kreuzeswissenschaft*, op. cit., pp. 96–97.

Usually, the stages are: through vocal prayer to meditation, then on to contemplative prayer. Edith Stein says: "As a fruit of meditation, a state of loving recognition is attained. The soul remains now in quiet, peaceful, loving self-surrender in the presence of God . . . without meditating on any particular truth of the faith." As a fruit of meditation, this kind of inner prayer is also called "acquired contemplation." But God does as he will and gives as he wishes. He can give someone interior prayer "directly," so to speak. "God can also grant the soul," Edith Stein notes, "a shadowy, loving awareness of himself even without any preliminary practice of meditation. He can suddenly place [the soul] in a state of contemplation and of love, and pour contemplation into [it]." Then a person feels himself suddenly "seized by the tangible presence of God."[15]

Contemplative prayer as a gift

Francis de Sales makes it clear that we can only receive such contemplative prayer as a gift. We can prepare ourselves for it, pray for it, but never simply "produce" it on our own. "It is not in our power to have it when we please, and it does not depend on our efforts, but God at his pleasure works it in us by his most holy grace."[16] Vocal prayer and meditation supply the wood that will receive the flame of the Holy Spirit. The spark that ignites the heart for interior prayer is a gift of God, a grace, which human prayer cannot force, but only request.

In prayer one meditates on the Word of God, speaks to Jesus, and looks upon him. But for prayer really to be an exchange of love, a true accepting and giving, and indeed

---

15. Stein, *Das Kreuz wie eine Krone tragen*, op. cit., 110.
16. Francis de Sales, *Treatise on the Love of God*, Bk. VI, Ch. 7, art. 1.

a simple resting in the tangible presence of God's love, is a gift of God. We are unable even to bring our ever-wandering thoughts to a state of rest. This, too, must be given to us. As the *Catechism* says of interior prayer: "It is a gift, a grace; it can be accepted only in humility and poverty" (CCC 2713).

Although vocal and meditative prayer are still present in interior prayer, silence, both of words and of thoughts, nevertheless begins to occupy a larger part of the time. This is silence as pure receptiveness and thereby, at the same time, as a giving of oneself. As long as I am active in prayer, by my thoughts or words, I can only receive in part. The more I attain to interior silence, the more God can communicate himself to me without hindrance.

Now prayer seems to become more and more passive. The activity of the one praying moves more into the background, while God's action moves increasingly to the fore. This is the prayer of our Lady: "Be it done unto me according to thy word" (Lk 1:38). Through this prayer, we allow God to act in us. We surrender ourselves to the action of the Holy Spirit. It is the Holy Spirit who prays within us (Rom 8:26), and the more we let him do that, the deeper our prayer becomes.

Francis de Sales and Teresa of Avila therefore speak of "the prayer of quiet." In this type of prayer, the soul is so "inwardly recollected in God or before God," "so sweetly attentive to the goodness of her well-beloved," that she notices "that her attention seems not to her to be attention, so purely and delicately is it exercised."[17] "Now this repose sometimes goes so deep in its tranquility, that the whole soul and all its powers fall as it were asleep, and make no

---

17. Ibid., Ch. 8, art. 2.

movement or action whatever."[18] If this prayer of quiet is given to us, St. Francis advises us to remain in it. "When you shall find yourself in this simple and pure filial confidence with our Lord, stay there, without moving yourself to make sensible acts, either of the understanding or of the will; for this simple love of confidence, and this love-sleep of your spirit in the arms of the Savior, contains by excellence all that you go seeking hither and thither to satisfy your taste."[19]

Thus a sign of this silent interior prayer granted by the Holy Spirit is a certain inability to pray in the usual, active way. Edith Stein says of it: "One's soul is no longer capable of producing understandable considerations or of formulating definite resolutions. She is quite seized by something that presses upon her irresistibly, which is the presence of her God, who is close to her and allows her to rest with him."[20]

When our Lord leads us into such contemplative prayer, we are at first confused. It can even happen that we feel a certain resistance to vocal prayer, to reading Holy Scripture, or to thinking about anything. We would rather simply be there in God's presence. That is our Lord's invitation to enter into the dialogue of silence. At such a moment it would be a mistake to return to vocal prayer or meditation. When the Holy Spirit, the teacher of prayer (CCC 2672), leads me to simple repose with the Lord, I should let myself be led. The danger is that we may at once 'crush' these preliminaries of the prayer of quiet by not following them and instead returning to activity, words, and meditation.

---

18. Ibid., art. 3.
19. Ibid., art. 9.
20. Edith Stein, *Das Kreuz wie eine Krone Tragen*, op. cit., 105.

To be sure, this doesn't mean activity in the form of vocal and meditative prayer is bad, but only that everything has its own time, as God leads us. It is precisely at the beginning of the way of prayer—and usually also of a time of prayer—that human activity is necessary. "Thou hast said, 'Seek ye my face.' My heart says to thee, 'Thy face, Lord, do I seek'" (Ps 27:8). We seek the Lord's face by recollecting ourselves, becoming aware of his presence, considering his words. But when we have found his face and rest in his gaze, we have reached the goal. We have nothing more to do but let him look at us and love us while we look at him and love him.

Interior prayer in the dynamism of love

The stillness of interior prayer is not empty silence. We allow ourselves to be filled by the Holy Spirit and are drawn into the love of God. Resting in love is never static, for one is drawn into the inner dynamic of divine love, the exchange of love among the three divine Persons. Many who pray describe this interior prayer not just as "resting" or "being silent" but as a movement of love, as jubilation, and dance. In the Psalms we read: "I keep the Lord always before me. . . . Therefore my heart is glad . . . in thy presence there is fullness of joy, in thy right hand are pleasures for evermore" (Ps 16:8–12). Mechthild von Magdeburg (1207–1271) experienced God's love as "flowing light." In one of her mystical dialogues, God invited her to dance, and she replied: "I can't dance, Lord, unless you lead me. If you want me to dance, you will have to sing a song, then I will leap with love. There I will stay and continue dancing."[21]

---

21. Mechthild von Magdeburg, *Das Fliessende Licht der Gottheit*, Bk. 1, Ch. 44.

In a hymn to the heart of Jesus, Paul Gerhardt sings:

Take away my heart, my highest good,
And lay it down, where your heart rests,
There it is in the best hands;
There it will go with you as to a dance,
There it will praise the glory of your house,
And will still not be able to praise enough.

(*Nimm hin mein Herz, mein höchstes Gut,*
und leg es hin, wo dein Herz ruht,
da ist's wohl aufgehoben;
da geht's mit dir gleich als zum Tanz,
da lob es deines Hauses Glanz
und kann's doch nicht g'nug loben.)[22]

The sense of these texts is that in contemplative prayer the prayer of stillness and the jubilation of praise are joined.

"Before all else, strive for love!"

Mystics like Francis de Sales, Teresa of Avila, and John of the Cross describe deep mystical experiences of union with Christ that they call "rapture," "ecstasy," "spiritual betrothal," or "spiritual marriage." These highest forms of contemplative prayer are not substantially different from what has so far been described. The difference resides in the strength and duration of the interior union with Christ.

---

22. Paul Gerhardt, *Hymne an das Herz Jesus*, "*O Herz des Königs aller Welt*," Str. 7, 1–6. In Paul Gerhardt, *Geistliche Lieder*, Gerhard Rödding, Stuttgart, 1991, 17.

Our Lord gives everyone the grace of prayer he or she needs. St. John of the Cross emphasizes that God does not grant such mystical experiences to everyone, and he makes it clear that holiness does not depend on them. Holiness is to be found not in the loftiest feelings of love but in poor and humble abandonment to the Father's loving will (CCC 2712).

Perfect prayer is therefore not the highest "states of prayer" but prayer that is a complete self-surrender to God's will. That includes accepting one's own poverty and ineptitude in prayer. To Sister Julitta Ritz (a mystic who lived in the last century in Würzburg), when she was reproaching herself because her prayer was so poor, Jesus said: "Don't keep asking yourself, 'What am I doing wrong?' . . . I want to be loved by you just as you are now."

It is normal to yearn for prayer in which we feel God's love. But while longing for it, we should not want to force it. "As the eyes of servants look to the hand of their master . . . so our eyes look to the Lord our God, till he have mercy upon us" (Ps 123:2). Our Lord knows best when and how to lead us by grace into inner prayer. "For man does not see God by his own powers; but when he pleases he is seen by men, by whom he wills, and when he wills, and as he wills."[23]

There is always a danger that longing for the tangible experience of God will be tainted with egotism—by a greater desire for the tangible experience than for the beloved himself. Lest we make this mistake, God leads us on the way of prayer through difficulties and purification.

---

23. Irenaeus of Lyons, *Adversus Haereses*, Bk. 4, Ch. 20, 5.

Chapter 4

DIFFICULTIES AND PURIFICATION IN PRAYER

"The great figures of prayer of the Old Covenant before Christ . . . and he himself, all teach us this: prayer is a battle" (CCC 2725). It is a battle with many aspects. First it is necessary to find time for prayer, and that can mean overcoming not only external hindrances and distractions, but inner ones: "I don't feel like it," "Right now I have this urgent job to finish," "First of all, I need a little relaxation. . . ." Often it seems as if prayer, "being unproductive, is useless" (CCC 2727). At other times it is simply love of comfort that keeps us from praying (CCC 2725).

"The 'spiritual battle' of the Christian's new life is inseparable from the battle of prayer" (CCC 2725). Prayer is for the spiritual life what breathing is for bodily life. Someone who no longer prays dies spiritually. Since prayer is indispensable, the battle to pray must be renewed daily, since there is someone who wants to draw us away from God. The battle of prayer cannot be avoided by anyone who wishes to live with Christ. Let us consider what this battle may look like and what weapons we have available to us.

1. Distractions

Having overcome the first barrier and taken time out for prayer, one customarily encounters a difficulty against which the *Catechism* warns: "The habitual difficulty in prayer is distraction" (CCC 2729).

I try to concentrate, but my thoughts wander here and there. I think of things that have happened or that still lie ahead, about joyful or sorrowful events, about people who are close to my heart, and people I find repellent. In the silence at the beginning of the prayer time it is normal to become aware of what inwardly concerns oneself. The question is how to deal with it. If it's a beautiful experience, can I recall that it was God who granted it to me, thank him for it, and thereby return to him? When a sorrow or an inner need troubles me, can I entrust it to our Lord, "bring my prayer with thanksgiving to God" (cf. Phil 4:6), and in this way return to him?

Thoughts like these, capable of being turned into prayer, aren't really distractions yet. They only become such when they go on occupying our thoughts and feelings—when we concentrate on them and not on our Lord. The problem isn't that they come to mind but that I retain them, unable to let them go. "A distraction reveals to us what we are attached to" (CCC 2729).[1]

What should one do when one must struggle with distractions? The *Catechism* advises us to have "humble awareness before the Lord" and "resolutely to offer him our heart to

---

1. This is how Teresa of Avila diagnosed it: "Without our noticing it right away, we suddenly find ourselves thinking of things that we are attached to." (*The Way of Perfection*, 19:7).

be purified" (CCC 2729). Difficulties in prayer point to the
stumbling blocks on our way to God—the matters regarding
which we still need conversion.

Upon becoming aware of a distraction, it's best simply
to return peacefully to our Lord and not attempt actively to
struggle against it. "To set about hunting down distractions
would be to fall into their trap, when all that is necessary
is to turn back to our heart" (CCC 2729). The virtue that
helps here is humility. For distractions reflect our weaknesses
of spirit, and humility means recognizing one's weakness—
"Lord, I can do so little by myself"—and remaining in peace.
Getting upset and losing peace in the face of distractions
shows that one hasn't yet deeply grasped how poor one is and
how little one can do by oneself. "The humble are not surprised by their distress; it leads them to trust more, to hold
fast in constancy" (CCC 2733).

While distractions are normal, we need to realize that
they're furthered by curiosity that wants to see and hear
everything. Someone who needlessly fills his or her mind with
everything on the TV or the radio or the chatter of neighbors
or colleagues at work can hardly be surprised at being unable
to concentrate in prayer. A recollected attitude that leads
one to skip exposure to unnecessary images and words is very
helpful in reducing distractions in prayer.

2. Temptations

Many different temptations are encountered in prayer. Once
the struggle to overcome inner and outer resistance is won
and you've begun a time of prayer, temptations will try to
make you cut short the time or give it up praying entirely.

When prayer is tedious and dry, it's easy to think, "a distracted prayer like this won't help. I'd rather pray tomorrow and make it longer and deeper." Longer and deeper means more satisfying emotionally, and when the emotional satisfaction doesn't come, we consider ourselves unable to pray and give it up.

The mistake here lies in believing that our intellect or emotions are reliable indicators of what God is working in us. Take comfort in the realization that our distractions are no obstacle to God's activity in us. No matter how poor we feel ourselves to be, God's work in us is far beyond what we can grasp by our intellect or feelings. And a dry period of prayer, endured only by an act of love and fidelity to God, can bear rich fruit. When a small child brings his parents a sheet of paper with a scribbled drawing and proudly presents it as a gift, it may not be particularly valuable from an artistic point of view, but the parents will still rejoice at this product of their child's effort and love. In the same way God rejoices over our prayer no matter how impoverished it is.

There is also a temptation to want to gauge just where we stand in relation to prayer. Was it "good" or "bad" today? Have we reached this or that "stage"? Beware of judging your prayer. In doing this, you are turning attention on yourself, and that leads away from prayer. Genuine prayer always is focused upon God. He looks at us and leads us in his wisdom, which far exceeds our small thoughts.

Another temptation can arise from the fact that the depths of the soul manifest themselves in prayer. We discover things in ourselves that frighten us, thoughts and impulses we would prefer to cover up and not see. The thought can arise:

"Since I've begun to pray regularly, I seem to have become worse rather than better." But it isn't so. What we're seeing now was there before—we just didn't see it because we couldn't bear seeing ourselves as we are. God has known that for a long time, and it doesn't horrify him or keep him from loving us. "God shows his love for us in that while we were yet sinners Christ died for us" (Rom 5:8). And it doesn't prevent him from loving us now. Only in the light of his merciful love can we slowly dare to look at all the impurity still in us and let it be taken away by his mercy.

The light of the Holy Spirit brings to the surface the deep egotism, pride, and other vices hidden in our hearts. "And when he [the Holy Spirit] comes, he will convince [reveal to] the world concerning sin" (Jn 16:9). The Spirit helps us see the truth about ourselves and admit that there is nothing good in us, nothing but poverty and sin. When we show our poverty to our Lord and allow the light of his mercy to shine on it, it is transformed into light. "When anything is exposed by the light it becomes visible, for anything that becomes visible is light" (Eph 5:13f). The path of prayer is a path into humility—that is, into knowing the truth about ourselves. God's intention is not to discourage us in this way but invite us to discover his still greater mercy and to accept it. The realization of our poverty is more and more transformed into praise of his mercy.

In order to pray, however, it is indispensable not only to be forgiven but to forgive. One must resist the temptation to be resentful and cling to one's anger. It's not uncommon precisely in a time of prayer to recall the wounds others have inflicted on us by words and deeds. Then we can withdraw into our sense of injury or expose it to the Lord's light and freely make an act of forgiveness. It may be—in fact, it's likely—that despite ourselves the same thing will trouble us again. But that freely willed act of forgiveness is decisive. All of it—the injury, the wound—have been opened up to our Lord. With time, he can send us healing and peace through the Holy Spirit. Though troubled feelings linger, we nevertheless are at peace.

Frightening, confusing temptations against faith can also assail us as we pray. Suddenly doubts arise: "Does God really hear me when I pray, or am I just speaking, altogether meaninglessly, to the air?" "Is Jesus really present in the consecrated Host, or am I just praying to a piece of bread?" St. Paul indicates a tactic to adopt against such attacks of the evil one in his letter to the Ephesians: "Take the shield of faith, with which you can quench all the flaming darts of the evil one. And take the helmet of salvation, and the sword of the Spirit, which is the word of God" (Eph 6:16–17). Trusting in the Word of God, I make an act of faith. I do just the opposite of what the temptation suggests to me. Here the position of one's body can be very important in expressing faith. So, for instance, I can deliberately kneel before the Host to express faith in Christ's real presence.

Temptations lead us to humility. They show us our weakness and poverty, and we realize that without God's grace we would not be strong enough to resist. Without him we can't do anything. And so we learn to depend more and more on him, not on our own strength. Inner peace is easily lost. Our Lord invites us to be at peace and humbly, smilingly bring our weakness before him and place our trust in him alone.

3. Dryness

Along with the difficulties caused by distractions and temptations, the *Catechism of the Catholic Church* speaks of "discouragement during periods of dryness" (CCC 2728). Dryness, also called aridity, refers to a condition in which the heart feels "separated from God, with no taste for thoughts, memories, and feelings, even spiritual ones" (CCC 2731). Dryness is also a kind of distaste for prayer. Feeling no inner joy, we struggle, with the impression of wasting our time. Our spirit resists thinking of God or meditating on a mystery of faith. Even if we don't completely abandon prayer, the time of prayer is taken up in battling distractions.

Dryness can have various causes—natural or supernatural, produced by us or sent by God for the purification and deepening of our prayer. Natural causes include illness and exhaustion, negligence or lukewarmness in the spiritual life. Among the spiritual defects are excessive attachments to things or persons, or spiritual pride that can lead to a slackening of prayer life.

Causes of dryness such as these are easily recognized. The only possible therapy is a sincere turning back to God—confessing one's fault and asking him, "Create in me a clean heart, O God, and put a new and right spirit within me. Restore to me the joy of thy salvation" (Ps 51:10, 12).

It may be, though, that we sincerely turn to our Lord but still experience nothing but dryness in our prayer. We seek our Lord, but nothing happens except our own poor efforts. Then it is easy to become discouraged in the face of dryness.

All spiritual teachers speak of this phase of inner dryness. They understand it as a way by which God deals with souls, something necessary for the purification of hearts. Jesus says as much in the Gospel of St. John: "Every branch that does bear fruit he prunes, that it may bear more fruit" (Jn 15:2). One should therefore be calm in the face of such periods of dryness and purification. They are necessary in order that prayer be purified of egotistic features and that we are led to ever more genuine love. According to John of the Cross, "beginners in the spiritual life" need to be purified of attachment to spiritual consolations, since their attitude is still very much "ignoble, and has much to do with their love of self and their own inclinations."[2]

What we have here is something like the difference between 'being in love' and loving. Being in love involves feelings of inebriation, and, perhaps without realizing it, a person in this state can in the beginning love the good feeling (and so himself or herself) more than the one who, for a limited period of time, arouses it. The test of love's genuineness is whether, after the elation passes, love for the other continues in ordinary life. Only there can love's depth be gauged.

John of the Cross describes this dryness, which he calls "the night of the senses," like this: "When they are going about these spiritual exercises with the greatest delight and pleasure, and when they believe that the sun of Divine favor is shining most brightly upon them, God turns all this light of theirs into darkness, and shuts against them the door and the

---

2. John of the Cross, *The Dark Night*, Bk. I, Ch. 8, 3.

source of the sweet spiritual water which they were tasting in God whensoever and for as long as they desired."[3] The night of the senses therefore means that we have no tangible joy in prayer, no tangible experience any longer of God's love.

How should we act at such times? Spiritual teachers advise us not to shorten our prayer in any case. The right course of action is to patiently endure the dryness. At such moments we realize very vividly that without God we can do nothing—not even pray. He permits us to experience our weakness. Rather than grow discouraged and giving up prayer, this is the time to give ourselves over to our Lord, expecting everything from him and nothing from ourselves.

When unable to pray in any other way, seek help in set forms of prayer. At times of dryness, oral prayers like the Our Father or the Rosary are often the only forms of prayer available to one.

Times of dryness are also opportunities for acts of pure love: "It is only through love that I am now remaining in prayer to you, O Lord." In this way we grow in love. It is normal that while many periods of prayer are satisfying to us, others seem to go nowhere. Then one must ask oneself, What do I seek in prayer, God's blessing or the God who blesses?[4]

St. Francis de Sales expressed the attitude of pure love like this: "I do not seek joys, but Him himself."[5] He illustrated this by the example of a deaf singer who is a lute player.[6] Since he

---

3. Ibid.

4. *Treatise on the Love of God*, Bk. VII, Ch. 3, 2.

5. Ibid.

6. See ibid., Bk. IX, Ch. 9, 1

is deaf, the singer no longer gets any joy from his lute playing. He plays only to please his prince. Now and then, though, the prince asks him to play when he himself is absent. Then the singer was also without the joy of pleasing his prince.

In this way Francis illustrated the ideal of pure love, to which a man is led little by little through the removal of human compensations. The lute player stands for the human heart. Ordinarily the singer hears the music—that is, the heart is comforted by the joy of loving God.[7] But "beginners in piety" are in danger of taking a different path without realizing it: "Instead of falling in love with God, they fall in love with the love they bear him."[8] Instead of seeking God, they turn back to themselves.[9] The sufferings of the soul during inner dryness are intended to correct this false attitude and bring one back to pure love. Though no longer finding any joy in loving, the heart shows the genuineness of its love by continuing to love without joy but only to please God.

But even the certainty of pleasing God without experiencing joy can be taken away from one, and this suffering is even harder to bear. "But when you turn your eyes from me, and I no longer perceive the sweet savor of the pleasure which you take in my song—truly God, what pangs my soul endures!"[10]

God doesn't will this inner suffering for its own sake but as a means of purifying this individual's love and freeing it

---

7. See ibid., Bk. IX, Ch. 9, 2.
8. Ibid., Bk. IX, Ch. 9, 3,
9. Cf. ibid., Bk. IX, Ch. 9, 4.
10. Ibid., Bk. IX, Ch. 11, 3.

from egotism. "Such then are the feelings of the soul which is in the midst of spiritual anguish. This purifies and refines love, for being deprived of all pleasure by which its love might be attached to God, it joins and unites us to God immediately, will to will, heart to heart, without any intervention of satis-faction or desire."[11]

Dryness in prayer is usually joined to a dryness in the active life. One's work or daily duties no longer bring the slightest joy. Everything becomes wearisome. The person asks: Why am I doing this—for my own satisfaction or out of love for others, for our Lord? Such times of dryness are an opportunity to act out of pure love and to purify one's action of all egoistical features—a time to decide knowingly to do everything only out of love for God, even though what is done gives not the slightest joy.

When we act in this way, we are really living in the Holy Spirit. As the fruit of acting from true love, we shall experi-ence the "fruits of the Spirit": a peace in the depths of the soul that only God can grant. If, in contrast, we are careless in our work, halfhearted and neglectful, we experience the "fruits of the flesh"—dissatisfaction, emptiness, sadness.

There are different kinds of dryness. It can extend to not only the emotional but also the intellectual realm. Then it becomes the "dark night" in which, so to speak, the light of faith is completely extinguished. Thérèse of Lisieux reported such times, when she "was in such a night that she did not know any more whether God still loved her."[12] Though she'd

---

11. Ibid., Bk. IX, Ch. 12, 4.
12. Thérèse of Lisieux, *Selbstbiographie*, Einsiedeln, 1996, 172.

had a strong faith from her early childhood, she spoke of "the thoughts of the worst materialists" pressing upon her spirit, denying God and the reality of eternal life: "You dream of a land of light . . . you dream that the Creator of these wonders will be yours forever, you think one day to escape from these mists where you now languish. Nay, rejoice in death, which will give you, not what you hope for, but a night darker still, the night of utter nothingness!"[13]

The dark night can cast a shadow over one's hope as well as one's faith. The soul is tortured by the thought "that God has abandoned it, and, in his abhorrence of it, has flung it into darkness . . . the feeling of God's absence, of being chastised and rejected by him . . . and even more, for now it seems that this affliction will last forever."[14]

The deepest purification of the soul takes place in the dark night. In these moments all that remains is either despair or a radical, naked faith: the leap of faith in the midst of surrounding darkness. The feeling of abandonment is the signal to abandon oneself and one's attachment to emotional or intellectual reassurances and give oneself over radically and solely to God. Such moments of darkness are a call to an act of perfect trust and self-surrender going far beyond what is possible in times of spiritual well-being.

"When Jesus hides himself, in this so sorrowful inner test of dryness, fear, and darkness; when all words of love and of trust no longer say anything to us, no longer touch us—that is the moment to go to the extreme in our faith. These trials are

---

13. Ibid., 221.
14. John of the Cross, *The Dark Night*, Bk. 2, Ch. 6, 2.

graces, since they are opportunities for pure faith. Pure love is realized in pure faith, and pure faith is realized in darkness."[15]

When we hold to our Lord with fidelity, the night really becomes a time of grace in which faith is deepened much more than in times of joy. Fidelity in darkness brings rich fruit, and after the time of darkness there surely comes the light of the Resurrection, a new joy and depth in prayer. In a certain way, the night of faith brings us a share in the inner path followed by Jesus himself: that sense of abandonment by God that he suffered on the Cross when he prayed: "My God, my God, why have you forsaken me?" And as the Passion was for him the way out of this world to his Father (Jn 13:1), so our path to the Father with Jesus passes through the darkness of the Cross, where the old man dies with Christ so that we can rise with him as a new man.

The *Catechism* says of the night of prayer: "This is the moment of sheer faith clinging faithfully to Jesus in his agony and in his tomb. 'Unless a grain of wheat falls into the earth and dies, it remains alone; but if it dies, it bears much fruit' (Jn 12:24). . . . The Paschal night of the resurrection passes through the night of the agony and the tomb" (CCC 2731, 2719).

Dryness and this night are thus necessary in the contemplative life so that God can cleanse us in the depths of the heart from all egoistical striving and from attachment to all that is not God. In this way he strengthens our faith and our love. Moreover, the endurance of the night of faith brings rich fruit not only for us but also for others. "Contemplative

---

15. Pére d'Elbée, *Croire à l'amour*, 103-104.

prayer is a communion of love—bearing life for the multitude, to the extent that it consents to abide in the night of faith" (CCC 2719). In the midst of her night of faith, Thérèse of Lisieux could write: "I tell Jesus, that I am happy, not to enjoy this beautiful Heaven here on earth, so that he might open it up to the poor unbelievers for eternity. Although this test robs me of every enjoyment of feelings, I can still call out: 'For thou, O Lord, hast made me glad by thy work; at the works of thy hands I sing for joy' (Ps 91)."[16]

---

16. Thérèse of Lisieux, op. cit., 222.

Chapter 5

CONTEMPLATION IN ORDINARY LIFE

Having considered the time of prayer and the difficulties encountered on the path of prayer, we now turn to contemplation in ordinary life. The time of prayer is important for living in a contemplative way, but prayer must continue into the ordinary life.

Prayer that continues in ordinary life plainly is different from prayer during the time of prayer. In the time of prayer, we are at liberty to direct the powers of memory, understanding, and will entirely to God. In ordinary life, we normally must focus our concentration and strength on the tasks that need carrying out. Nevertheless, we can pray continually in the midst of ordinary life though in a different way.

1. Aspirations

Aside from the times that we expressly set aside for prayer, everyday life has many moments when our attention is not fully and unreservedly directed to working—for example, on the way to work or while waiting for the computer to do something or waiting to be connected to someone on the telephone. Such moments can be put to good use by praying. If you pause and think about it, every single day affords many such opportunities to raise one's heart briefly to God. St. John Chrysostom made that point back in the fourth century: "Even in the market place or on a walk alone, it is possible to pray often and fervently. Also when you are sitting in your business or are buying or selling, yes, even while cooking."[1]

Prayers of this sort used to be called "ejaculatory prayers." Spiritual writers like St. Francis de Sales strongly recommended them. They are a good way of constantly renewing one's unity with God: "One can also maintain unity with God through short and fleeting but frequent raising of the heart to God, by praying aspirations."[2] These aspirations "can supply all other deficiencies, but there is hardly any means of making up where this is lacking."[3] Their value lies in maintaining unity with God in the midst of ordinary life.

Little reminders—to remain in prayer and to use small pauses in activity for prayer—can be helpful. Many people set their watches or clocks to ring or beep softly on the hour as a reminder for them to pray. A small icon or image on one's desk or worktable can help remind one of God from time to time.

As is usual in a life of prayer, here too it's the rule that our efforts are necessary (cf. CCC 2725) and also that a continual

---

1. Cited in CCC 2743.
2. *Treatise on the Love of God*, Bk. VII, Ch. 4, 8.
3. Francis de Sales, *Introduction to the Devout Life*, Part II, Ch. 13.

union with our Lord in ordinary life is always a gift of the Holy
Spirit. He prays within us; and in these moments when the
intellect is free, conscious prayer comes to mind almost as if
by itself. St. Ignatius of Antioch wrote: "Living and speaking
water is in me. It says to me: Go to the Father."[4] Our task is
to listen to the Spirit praying within us and unite ourselves
to that prayer. As is usually the case in the way of prayer, this
requires more effort at the start. With time, we become aware
that it is the Holy Spirit who prays in us and helps us remain
in the state of inner prayer.

Different kinds of aspirations help us to remain in prayer.
Now we shall look more closely at some.

2. Prayers of Praise

The Psalms summon us to praise God at every moment: "I
will bless the Lord at all times; his praise shall continually
be in my mouth" (Ps 34:2). Practicing that continual prayer
of praise becomes possible upon discovering that there is
reason to glorify God in every event of daily life, joyful or
troubling, in the certainty that "in everything God works for
good with those who love him" (Rom 8:28). Everything can
be an invitation to prayer. Prayer of praise transforms the
way one sees ordinary life, strengthens faith, and enables
one to live every moment in full trust and joyful self-surrender
to the Lord.[5]

---

4. St. Ignatius of Antioch, *Epistle to the Romans*, 7, 2.
5. Cf. *Handbook of the Community of Emmanuel*, 1, 20.

3. The Jesus prayer

The "Jesus prayer," also known as the "Prayer of the Heart," is used especially in the Eastern Churches. A simple prayer, such as "Lord Jesus, have mercy on me," is associated with breathing or even with the beating of the heart. It is not the words that are essential, but the union with Jesus.

This prayer can also take other forms prompted by God, for example, "Jesus, Thou in me and I in Thee," or "Jesus, my Lord and my God." A phrase from Holy Scripture can be used this way. St. Francis de Sales recommended assembling a "spiritual bouquet" at the conclusion of every period of prayer[6]—that is, summing up the thoughts and words given in this time of prayer by our Lord. One "flower"—a word or two that struck us most deeply during prayer—can then be used as the aspiration or Jesus prayer of that day. The first Psalm asks us to think about God's word "day and night"—in other words, always. The word used for "thinking about" could also mean murmur or repeat softly. Thus, in repeating a word our Lord has given us in our heart, we remain in union with the Word of God, with Jesus.

4. Prayers for everyday activities

Finally, there can be particular prayers to accompany everyday activities. Even the most ordinary activities can lead to prayer. For example, upon getting up, one can say a prayer like: "Praise to you, almighty Father, for your mercy is renewed

---

6. *Treatise on the Love of God*, Bk. II, 7.

every day. Let me arise from the dead, Christ my savior is my light." Leaving home in the morning: "Praise to you, almighty Father. You protect me when I leave and return. Let me stay with you wherever I am."

Individuals can make up their own prayers. What's important is that the prayers help them carry out their daily activities in the presence of God.

5. Attentiveness to moments of grace

A further aspect of contemplative life in the midst of the everyday is attentiveness for visits by God. Rather than we consciously deciding to pray (as in the case of aspirations), God calls the soul to himself in the midst of what we're doing. This can take different forms: the experience of a peace deep in the soul, a longing for God, an insight, new light concerning something to be done or said. When these impulses are only slight and unclear, as sometimes happens, it is all the more important to pay attention and allow oneself to be drawn along.

Thérèse of Lisieux said: "I know he is within me. He is there, always guiding and inspiring me; and just when I need them, lights, hitherto unseen, break in. This is not as a rule during my prayers, but in the midst of my daily duties."[7] God speaks throughout the day, not only during times of prayer. As Vatican II's *Constitution on Divine Revelation* says, he is "continually in converse with the spouse of his beloved Son"

---

7. Thérèse of Lisieux, op. cit., 185.

(*Dei Verbum*, 8), that is, with the Church and with each of us. It's up to us to hear his voice and enter into this "continuing conversation."

6. Contemplative in action

- Although there are pauses in daily work that can be used for prayer, moments of grace when we are aware of God's presence, for most of the day one's attention is centered on the work to be done. So how can a person ensure that work itself will help him or her to remain with God?

- Part of the answer resides in the fact that there are quite different ways of doing what one does. It is possible to become so absorbed in a task that inner recollection is lost. That is the failing Jesus called to Martha's attention. He didn't criticize her for serving him—that was a true work of love of neighbor. But he did complain that she "was distracted with much serving" (Lk 10:40)—so taken up with it that she was no longer interiorly available for a personal encounter with him. Indeed, the Church Fathers have understood this biblical story as a call to join contemplative life and active life—not to let oneself be completely taken up with exterior tasks, even in the midst of business, but to maintain an inner distance and, like Mary, interiorly sit at the feet of the Lord.

- To remain with God in the midst of activity, it helps to place the activity in the context of prayer. Before beginning, say a short prayer dedicating what will be done to our Lord: "Lord, I want to do this task with you and in you. Let it succeed to your honor and the benefit of mankind." Afterward, thank the Lord and return the results of our efforts (however they've turned out) to him. A simple prayer like this changes much. Instead of making the effort alone—even with the best of intentions, "for the Lord"—we work in him and with him. Jesus didn't say: "Work for me!" but, "Remain in me." He wants us to do things not just *for* him but *with* and *in* him. Particularly in tasks that demand full concentration and therefore do not allow simultaneous conscious prayer, it's important to pray before and after and so stay with the Lord in the midst of what is done.

According to St. John the Evangelist, God remains in us when we remain in his love (1 Jn 4:12). I can do the same work "because I have to" or out of love. I can head off to my job in the morning because the job requires it or out of love for those for whom I am working and for the family my work supports. A mother can make her children's beds because it's her duty or for love for the children whose pillows she fluffs. It's the same work, yet worlds apart. St. Paul tells us, "Let all that you do be done in love" (1 Cor 16:14). "God is love, and he who abides in love abides in God, and God abides in him" (1 Jn 4:16). When we abide in love, we live contemplatively, though in the midst of everyday activity.

In this way, activity itself becomes love and so, in a certain sense, prayer. In a sermon explaining St. Paul's exhortation to "pray without ceasing," St. Augustine said that "good works are the continuation of verbal prayer; and praying means entering into the love of the Trinity—receiving the Father's love and, with the Son, loving the Father. But loving means not only "love in word or speech but in deed and in truth" (1 Jn 3:18), that is, doing the will of God out of love for him. Action and contemplation are joined in love. St. Francis de Sales called prayer "affective" love and action "effective" love. Real prayer turns into action while remaining as prayer in love. Blessed Teresa of Calcutta told her sisters: "We are with Jesus for twenty-four hours, whether this is in the Eucharist or in the sick."

All true contemplation has an inner dynamism that leads to right action. Not busy action, but doing of what is seen in prayer to be God's will. Contemplation and action are not competitors but permeate one another. In the action that comes from prayer we are continuing our prayer, and we remain in God insofar as we do his will. This is something Jesus recommended in saying, "If you keep my commandments, you will abide in my love, just as I have kept my Father's commandments and abide in his love" (Jn 15:10). Only actions not oriented toward the will of God, or even opposed to him, hinder the maintaining of union with Christ that is central to the life of contemplation.

The link between action and contemplation can be seen in the life of Jesus. After a night spent in prayer, he decided to preach the Gospel in other cities (Lk 4:42–43) or call apostles to follow him (Lk 6:12–13). In prayer he sought the will of the Father, which he carried out in his life in obedience to love. "Jesus Christ was equal to God, but did not count equality with God a thing to be grasped, but emptied himself, taking the form of a servant . . . and became obedient unto death, even death on a cross" (Phil 6:12–13). The contemplative life, life in Trinitarian love, is thus not a comfortable relaxing in the experience of loving and being loved. More and more it takes on the contours of Jesus' life, which led him to its obedient giving up. Thus contemplative life involves prosaic obedience in doing one's daily tasks. Mary's words "Let it be to me according to your word" (Lk 1:38) were fulfilled in her daily care for Jesus. The *Magnificat* expresses Mary's jubilation at God's merciful love, and also her daily dedication to her motherly duties, which surely didn't always cause her to feel elated. Unity with Jesus in the will of his Father brought her to stand on Calvary beneath the cross.

"To live on love," says a poem by Thérèse of Lisieux, " 'tis not to fix one's tent / On Tabor's height and there with thee remain. / 'Tis to climb Calvary with strength nigh spent, / And count thy heavy cross our truest gain. . . . To live on love, 'tis without stint to give, / And never count the cost, nor ask reward."[8] Yet just this prosaic self-surrender is the path that leads to true joy. This is how Thérèse experienced it: "Yes, I felt love permeating my heart, the need to forget myself, in order to bring joy to others, and from then on I was happy."[9]

7. Union of hearts

The time of prayer, aspirations, the effort to do all things in and through love—all this will lead to an ever—deeper union of hearts with God. We cannot always concentrate on prayer,

---

8. *Poems of St. Thérèse, Carmelite of Lisieux*, trans. by S. L. Emery.
9. Thérèse of Lisieux, op. cit., 97.

since we need concentration for our tasks. We also need time
for relaxation, in order to restore our spiritual strength. But
we can pray in these times too and in fact do so through a
continual union with our Lord in the depths of the heart.
Prayer means union of love with God, and the place of this
union is deep in the heart. That is where we accept his love
and give ourselves to him. The communion of love in this
depth of the heart can also be maintained when the activities
of the day require external attention. Also, when the intellect
(the higher level of the spirit, so to speak) is busy with other
things, the depths of the heart (a much deeper-lying level of
the spirit) can remain untouched by them. This is how one
can be united with God interiorly even when externally busy
with other things.

Consider human love. If I love a person, he or she is
always present, even though physically absent. Love gives
all one's daily doings a different tone. Even though not consciously thinking of or speaking with the person, I am still
united to him or her.

St. Augustine made this observation regarding friendship.
You're always united with your friend even though physically
apart. Even when direct contact is impossible for a rather long
time, there is a real union of hearts. It's like that where union
with God is concerned. Engaged in external activity, one lives
in this interior union of hearts; and as soon as possible one
seeks, as in the case of friendship, to resume a direct contact
with our Lord in time dedicated to prayer.

How do we know we're moving toward unity of hearts with
our Lord? One sign is that when something important happens,

one thinks almost automatically of God and talks it over with him. That is an indication of being linked to him deep at heart even though other matters occupy one's attention.

Or, perhaps one hasn't thought consciously of God for quite a while because one's attention is otherwise engaged. When somebody asks one to do something to which our Lord would object, one spontaneously protests: unity with him in one's heart is still there.

Chapter 6

THE EFFECTS OF CONTEMPLATIVE LIFE

The concrete effects of contemplative life are immense. Only a life of constant inner prayer leads us into the full realization of our Christian vocation. Only through inner prayer can the word of God and the sacraments have their full effect on us. Only through prayer without ceasing will daily life be a manifestation of new life in the Holy Spirit. Let us consider these effects of prayer more closely.

1. A deepening of sacramental life

Prayer is something like the water plants need to grow. Seeds planted in dry earth and not watered won't germinate. The Word of God and the sacraments are seeds of divine grace that God plants in us. But they will remain without effect unless prayer creates an environment in which they can grow and bring forth fruit.

Confession. Only in prayer, through the light of the Holy Spirit, do we become aware of the extent of our inner poverty.

God himself shows us our faults and sins, all that "rubbish" stored, often unknowingly, in the soul. In confession one takes this rubbish to the garbage dump and finally is rid of it.

No matter how clearly we speak of it to another human being, we aren't really free of it. Only when God forgives are we truly freed of our guilt. "When I declared not my sin, my body wasted away through my groaning all day long. For day and night thy hand was heavy upon me; my strength was dried up as by the heat of summer. I acknowledged my sin to thee, and I did not hide my iniquity; I said, 'I will confess my transgressions to the Lord'; then thou didst forgive the guilt of my sin" (Ps 32:3–5).

This divine power of forgiveness was given to the apostles and through them to the Church, after his resurrection: "If you forgive the sins of any, they are forgiven; if you retain the sins of any, they are retained" (Jn 20:23). In this way we can really receive divine forgiveness in the Sacrament of Reconciliation, and through it we become a "new creation in Christ" (cf. 2 Cor 5:17). Forgiveness removes what separates us from God. It gives us through the Spirit new clarity of sight, untroubled joy in the heart, and new vivifying strength in the soul. "Restore to me the joy of thy salvation, and uphold me with a willing spirit. . . . Deliver me from blood guiltiness, O God, thou God of my salvation, and my tongue will sing aloud of thy deliverance" (Ps 51:12, 14). Prayer and Confession interact. God shows us in prayer the sins of which he wants to purify us, and he takes them away in Confession and thereby grants us a deeper union with him in prayer.

The Eucharist. To live once more in the Lord there is no more effective means than the Eucharist. "Abide in me, and I in you" (Jn 15:4). These words of Christ sum up contemplative life. Through the Eucharist the Lord, who is substantially present, comes to us in order to remain with us. "He who eats my flesh and drinks my blood abides in me, and I in him" (Jn 6:56). This is why it is so important how we receive our Lord in communion and spend time in prayer afterwards.

St. Teresa of Avila told her spiritual daughters: "Do not lose such an excellent time for talking with Him as the hour after Communion. Be very careful not to lose it. If you are compelled by obedience to do something else, try to leave your soul with the Lord. For he is your Master, and, though it be in a way you may not understand, he will not fail to teach you. But if you take your thoughts elsewhere, and pay no more attention to him than if you had not received him, and care nothing for his being within you, how can he make himself known to you? This, then, is a good time for our Master to teach us and for us to listen to him. This is the moment to ask him never to leave us."[1] The more deeply we enter into the experience of receiving our Lord in Communion, the more strongly his presence will accompany us throughout the whole day.

John Paul II wrote in his *Encyclical on the Eucharist*: "What more could Jesus have done for us? Truly, in the Eucharist, he shows us a love which goes 'to the end' (cf. Jn 13:1), a love which knows no measure. . . . In the Eucharist we have Jesus, we have his redemptive sacrifice, we have his

---

1. Teresa of Avila, *The Way of Perfection*, Ch. 34.

resurrection, we have the gift of the Holy Spirit, we have adoration, obedience, and love of the Father."[2]

As in the case of confession, there is also a relationship
between prayer and the Eucharist. Prayer brings us more
deeply into the mystery of the Eucharist, and the Eucharist
sacramentally renews our unity with Christ. In a poem Edith
Stein describes how receiving the Eucharist leads to a lasting
union of hearts with our Lord.

> Your Body mysteriously permeates my own,
> And your Soul unites itself with mine:
> I am no longer what I was before.
> You come and go, but the seed remains
> That you did sow of future splendor,
> Buried in this body of dust.
> A glint of heaven remains within the soul,
> A deep glow is seen within the eyes,
> A soaring in the sound of voice.
> The bond that fastens heart to heart remains,
> The stream of life, that springs forth from you
> And enlivens every limb.[3]

2. Effective action

Not only does inner prayer deepen our sacramental life, but
when we "pray always," prayer saturates our daily activities

---

2. John Paul II, Encyclical *Ecclesia de Eucharista*, 11 and 60.

3. Edith Stein, Gedicht *"Ich bleibe bei euch"* in *Verborgenes Leben* (ESW XI), 173.

and work. It enables us to see more clearly what we should be doing. It orients our action and protects us from excessive activism. For in prayer we learn what is really important and what we should do now. And so the contemplative life helps us avoid wasting time on unimportant things and set the right priorities. Thus the investment of time in daily prayer repays us many times over. Many people say, "I have no time for prayer." If they started praying, they would find time suddenly given to them, because prayer helps them to work more efficiently.

It is clear from the lives of the saints that an intense prayer life doesn't reduce output but actually increases it. In his biography of his teacher Albert the Great, St. Thomas Aquinas wrote: "It was only through his interior prayer that he was able to carry out his immense volume of work." When you see how much many saints accomplished—all their preaching and writing—it becomes obvious: Interior prayer does not subtract time from us, but gives us time, empowering us to do things far beyond what seems humanly possible.

As a result of inner prayer we come to work more effec-tively, for we are working and living in the strength of the Holy Spirit. This Spirit permeates not only our work but every moment of the day, leading us to the fullness of our Christian vocation: Life in and through the Holy Spirit.

3. Life in the Holy Spirit

That is what contemplative life is: life in the Holy Spirit. "By this we know that we abide in him and he in us, because he has given us of his own Spirit" (1 Jn 4:13). We can recognize this presence of the Holy Spirit in us. To be sure, as a divine

Person he is hidden and intangible; but we can recognize his working in us. Jesus likens the Spirit to the wind: "The wind blows where it wills, and you hear the sound of it, but you do not know whence it comes or whither it goes" (Jn 3:8). The wind itself can't be seen, but its effects on us and on others are visible. These effects of the Holy Spirit in us are manifold. A list (among others) of the fruits of the Holy Spirit is given by St. Paul in his letter to the Galatians: "The fruit of the Spirit is love, joy, peace, patience, kindness, goodness, faithfulness, gentleness, self-control" (Gal 5:22–23).

Let us take a closer look at three of these fruits of the Holy Spirit.

Love. Only through interior prayer can we carry out Jesus' command to love *all* men properly, including enemies. Acting according to our human feelings, we would be drawn to only some—relatively few—people. We would be indifferent to others and would more or less strongly dislike still others. In contemplative life, however, "we regard no one from a human point of view" (2 Cor 5:16). Instead we adopt God's view and way of acting. "Then I learn to look on this other person not simply with my eyes and my feelings, but from the perspective of Jesus Christ. His friend is my friend."[4] This is the "new commandment": "Love one another as I have loved you" (Jn 15:12). What is new in this is not loving one's neighbor as such, but that with this commandment God gives us the strength to fulfill it by himself remaining in us and loving the other.

---

4. Benedict XVI, *Deus Caritas Est*, no. 18.

Our emotions, our feelings, are purified by the Holy Spirit's strength acting in us. The attachment and egotism that move us to seek in others mainly what we can get for ourselves are diminished. Our natural inclinations become purer and stronger. "A heart that gives itself to God does not lose its natural tenderness; quite the opposite, this tenderness grows the purer and more godlike it becomes."[5]

We are thus enabled to overcome our antipathy to the other, inasmuch as we accept him or her for Jesus' sake, as Christ has accepted us, for the glory of God (cf. Rom 15:7). Thérèse of Lisieux offers an example from her life in the cloister: "There was in the community a sister, who had a talent for displeasing me in every respect: her manners, her words, her character seemed very unpleasant to me. But she was still a holy nun, who was certainly very pleasing to our dear God; so I did not want to give in to the natural antipathy that I felt. I said to myself that love must not be based on feelings, but must show itself in deeds: so I made the effort to do for this sister what I would have done for the person who was dearest to me. . . . One day she said to me with a beaming face: 'My dear Sister Thérèse, tell me what attraction you find in me, for whenever we meet, you greet me with such a sweet smile.' Ah! What attracted me was Jesus hidden in the depths of her soul—Jesus who makes sweet even that which is most bitter."[6]

Inner prayer enables us to become aware of the presence of Jesus in others. We see and accept them in a completely

---

5. Thérèse of Lisieux, op. cit., 225.
6. Ibid., 235f.

new way. "As you did it to one of the least of these my brethren, you did it to me" (Mt 25:40).

Joy. St. Paul never tired of saying, "Rejoice in the Lord always; again I will say, Rejoice" (Phil 4:4). He is speaking of something more than ordinary human joy—joy "in the Lord," joy which, no matter what situation we are in, springs from our being in him and he in us. That makes it possible "at all times," even in circumstances in which, from a human point of view, there is no basis for joy. St. Paul himself is an illustration of that, for when he wrote this letter, he was in prison. Yet he still could write this way about joy.

Jesus spoke in his high priestly prayer of inner communion with his Father and with his disciples, and he said, "These things I speak in the world, that they may have my joy fulfilled in themselves" (Jn 17:13). Joy in the Holy Spirit is Jesus' own joy at being infinitely loved by the Father and loving the Father. No one and nothing can take it from us. If, however, joy depends only on external events (which we can naturally also rejoice in), a time will certainly come when there is no longer a basis for joy. Someone who doesn't know the source of inner joy and cannot draw on it is then in danger of being overwhelmed by sadness from outside of him.

Christian joy and praise, expressions of "joy in the Lord," are nourished by two sources: God's *action* for our salvation and his *being*, which is love. Joy based on the story of salvation—that is, joy over what God has done—breaks out spontaneously when his deeds are revealed to us. "Sing to the

Lord, for he has triumphed gloriously" (Ex 15:21). So sings Miriam after the saving of Israel at the Red Sea.

This joy is also possible, however, in those moments when God's action is hidden and mysterious, indeed, often not understandable. Though apparently he had no reason for joy, the Prophet Habakkuk found joy in the Lord in faith: "Though the fig tree do not blossom, nor fruit be on the vines, the produce of the olive fail and the fields yield no food, the flock be cut off from the fold and there be no herd in the stalls, yet I will rejoice in the Lord, I will joy in the God of my salvation" (Hab 3:17–18).

Joy and praise can break out simply from looking at the being of God—how he is, how he loves us. The love of the groom in the Song of Songs is the basis for uninterrupted praise: "We will exult and rejoice in you; we will extol your love more than wine" (Song 1:4). One enters into this joy simply by looking at God by an act of faith. The natural response to looking at this "love to the end" (Jn 13:1) and abiding in love (1 Jn 4:16) is joy and praise. If I "keep the Lord always before me" (Ps 16:8), I can also say to him: "In thy presence there is fullness of joy, in thy right hand are pleasures for evermore" (Ps 16:11).

Peace. "We know that in everything God works for good with those who love him" (Rom 8:28).

Unexpected or undesired events often rob us of our inner peace. We have our own ideas about things—and then it all turns out differently. Only by remaining in God, and he in us, can we feel confident of his providence, accept it, and thus remain at peace.

Translated word for word from the Greek, verse 28 of the Epistle to the Romans says: "We know that for those who love God, everything cooperates for the good." God can make everything, even pain, sorrow, and guilt (which God doesn't want either) cooperate for our welfare. It is his almighty power at work. He can make something out of anything. He does not take our freedom from us—even when we misuse it against his will and damage ourselves and others. But he has the power to make even the worst deed cooperate for our good. This wonderful omnipotence of God is seen most clearly in the cross of Jesus. Here the greatest crime of mankind is transformed through his much greater love into the act of salvation for all.

In this world, with good reason, we are often in sorrow and fear. We constantly face new difficulties and problems. We Christians are no different in this from everyone else. The only difference is that Christians know about Christ's greater power and so despite all afflictions, can maintain their peace: "I have said this to you, that in me you may have peace. In the world you have tribulation; but be of good cheer, I have overcome the world" (Jn 16:33).

The basis for this peace is the knowledge that we live constantly protected in the hands of Jesus and thus in the almighty and loving hands of the Father. "[My sheep] shall never perish, and no one shall snatch them out of my hand. My Father, who has given them to me, is greater than all, and no one is able to snatch them out of the Father's hand" (Jn 10:28–29). The life of contemplation enables us to live in this faith at every moment and thereby in inner peace. It empowers us to rise above the merely "human" response to daily events, by which one falls immediately into unease or distress, and instead remain in peace, trusting in the guidance of God, whose ways are as far above our ways as heaven is above the earth (cf. Is 55:9). We can leave our wishes and notions, even our very lives, to him. He knows better than we what is good for us, and he cares for us (cf. 1 Pet 5:7)

Our failings and sins are another reason why we lose our inner peace. To fail at what we so often have attempted discourages us. If we remain in prayer (or, at least, return to it after being away from it), we shall see that this reaction doesn't conform to God's will. Yes, we need to have remorse for our sins so that we interiorly turn away from them. But that is only the first step. Having made this act of contrition, we can in the same moment appreciate God's infinite mercy toward us—and maintain our peace. Brother Lawrence of the Resurrection, a Carmelite of the seventeenth century, says of himself: "I feel very strongly the magnitude of my sins. But these do not discourage me. I confess them before God, I do not defend myself before him and do not seek an excuse. Then I return peacefully back to my ordinary works of love and adoration."[7] Remaining at odds with oneself comes either from refusing to let go of one's own injured pride ("That such a thing could happen to *me!*") or not esteeming highly enough God's mercy. Our weakness will not separate us from God if we only entrust ourselves immediately to his mercy.

---

7. *www.carmel.asso.fr/visages/laurent/ecrits-shtml-, florilège de texts.*

One who sets out on the way of contemplative life, little by little finds the way to this peace. Purely human reactions often come first. Only later, perhaps in the time of prayer, does God invite us, in this situation also, to entrust ourselves to his providence and remain in peace. The more we succeed in "praying without ceasing" the more spontaneous and "natural" will this supernatural reaction of faith become.

Conclusion

J esus always speaks about prayer in very simple words. He did not leave a difficult textbook to his disciples. He invited them to pray like children and call God "Father." If we take the path of childlike simplicity in prayer, God himself will lead us and reveal himself to us.

"I thank thee, Father, Lord of heaven and earth, that thou hast hidden these things from the wise and understanding and revealed them to babes" (Mt 11:25). Many of the great teachers of prayer never studied theology—God instructed them.

It was said above that to begin the way of prayer and remain faithful to it in times of dryness, we must long for it. But much greater than our longing for companionship with God could ever be, is God's longing for us! Constantly he calls us anew to seek his face (cf. Ps 27:8) and pray without ceasing, for he longs to give himself to us. He longs to be with us forever, to remain in us, to open to us the fullness of his love.

God's promise is our assurance. If we long for unbroken communion with him and ask him for it, he will give it to us: "For every one who asks receives, and he who seeks finds, and to him who knocks it will be opened" (Lk 11:10).

248.4